THE GROWTH BOOK

**This book is dedicated to my wife
Dorothy whose faith, hope and love
have sustained me in Christian ministry.**

THE
GROWTH
BOOK

by
Roy Pointer

MARC Europe
British Church Growth Association
BMMF Interserve

British Library Cataloguing in Publication Data
Pointer, Roy
  The growth book.
  1. Evangelistic work
  I. Title
  269'.2   BV3790

  ISBN 0–947697–27–6

First published 1987.
ISBN 0–947697–27–6
Typeset in Britain for MARC Europe, Cosmos House, 6 Homesdale Rd,
Bromley, Kent BR2 9EX by Input Typesetting Ltd, London, SW19 8DR,
and printed by Anchor Brendon Ltd, Tiptree, Colchester, Essex, CO5 0HD.

Contents

Preface

In 1978 the Bible and Medical Missionary Fellowship (BMMF Interserve) published a workbook, compiled by Robin Thomson, called *Can British Churches Grow?* It was a bold initiative that introduced Church Growth principles to many British ministers and church leaders. Robin and the BMMF are to be congratulated on the splendid work they did, and I consider it a privilege to be asked to write a follow-up to that workbook.

There are a number of changes in *The Growth Book*, from the style and format of *Can British Churches Grow?* First, we know that the British Church can grow and that some churches of every denomination are growing numerically. We also know that churches are growing in every county of England. There is therefore an increasing expectation of growth in the United Kingdom today. Because of this climate of expectation I have not considered it necessary to make a case for Church Growth or to be apologetic. I am also assuming that all who purchase and use this book are already convinced of the need to see their churches grow or grow more rapidly.

Secondly, I have written with the local church council and house group in mind. Thus this book is suitable for the ordinary church member who is willing to study the life and work of his church with a small group of fellow church members. Therefore the book is not scholarly, although I hope it is soundly based on the Scriptures and good scholarship. You will also discover that the book is not exhaustive on the subject of Church Growth. Further reading is suggested for those who wish to study Church Growth principles at greater depth.

Thirdly, this book is primarily designed to create a climate for growth by helping a group of Christians examine together the life and witness of their church in the light of God's Word and under the prompting of the Holy Spirit. I have attempted to write without bias toward a particular churchmanship or theological emphasis, and have also had an international readership in mind. Please forgive me if I have failed to be sensitive to your particular tradition or denomination. I pray that despite my attempted neutrality you will find sufficient relevant material to be able to make the necessary adjustments in language or emphasis so that this book is useful to your church.

Throughout the book I have used Church Growth (with the capital letters) to describe the formally defined 'school of missiology' of the Church Growth movement. This represents a growing body of research and literature essentially concerned with overcoming the obstacles to and promoting the cause of making disciples of all the peoples of the earth.

I pray that this book will enable all who use it to hear what the Spirit is saying to their church. For apart from the agency of the Holy Spirit there can be no true church growth, and all our endeavours to build the Body of Christ will be in vain.

Roy Pointer

Leader's Instructions
(That all may read!)

General Instructions

Please read the Preface before you read further. You will discover from the Preface that *The Growth Book* assumes you are committed to and concerned for the growth of your church.

I have no way of knowing how you, as the leader of the group, will use this book. I have written with the ordinary church member in mind and assumed that he or she is sufficiently committed to join a house group or accept leadership roles within the church. In other words I am assuming a degree of spiritual maturity, Christian commitment and knowledge of the Bible. Only you know the people in your group and to what extent you will have to expand or explain the material.

In an attempt to make this book usable by all denominations, I have avoided religious jargon and particular emphases – once again I assume you will adjust!

There are no times allocated for each session, and you may wish to study a session on one or more occasions. As you proceed through the sessions, some may be more relevant to your church than others, and therefore you may want to spend extra time on them.

I have used the words 'individual', 'group' or 'buzz groups' as group dynamic signals for you to follow, but you will need to apply them consistently to the group in which you choose to use this book. Flexibility has been my concern, so please feel free to adapt the material to suit yourself!

Some exercises in preparation for group discussion are requested to be done by the 'individual' alone. By 'group' I mean a gathering of about 12 people. 'Buzz groups' are of 2 to 4 people formed out of the group. If you have a group of less than 12 you may wish to ignore the 'buzz group' signal, but this size of group can often improve participation and discussion, if time and the meeting place allow. Whether or not group discussions and decisions are reported to a larger group or to the whole church depends on you (or the minister). If you have a very large group meeting in a church hall, for example, and divide it into groups of about 12 and/or buzz groups, you may wish to draw everything together at the end of each session. Instructions about suitable groups for the activities are given as suggestions.

The Growth Objective for each session is very important. This is what you set out to achieve for each study. You may wish to ask the group at the end of each session if the objective was achieved!

Prayers at the beginning of each session have been given themes from the Scriptures. These are only suggestions, as I have assumed you will provide the vitally important opening and closing devotions for each session.

The Leader's Time is your teaching time, when I expect you to introduce the new topic or activity or provide information. I am assuming you will read out loud and make these contributions to the group during the Leader's Time, and have written as if you were speaking. I hope you are happy with the script! *Notes* provide instructions for you to follow.

Bible references are given throughout for your use, if desired. Use whichever version you like. You may also want to add more biblical or other material to your presentations.

The Before Next Session sections are important home assignments to be completed if the next session is to be effective. You must stress the importance of these assignments and read them carefully to the group. Make sure everyone knows what he or she has to do. Check that they have been done as well as possible at the beginning of the next session.

It is important to make sure you have all equipment, such as a blackboard, flipchart or overhead projector, ready for each session. You, as the leader, will need sufficient copies of *The Growth Book* for every group member and a supply of Bibles, pencils and paper on hand. Photocopying any part of this book is an infringement of copyright, please don't forget!

Session Instructions

For All Sessions

Check list

Copies of *The Growth Book*   ☐

Equipment, blackboard stand for a flipchart, over-   ☐
head projector, etc.

Bibles   ☐

Pencils, paper, something to rest on   ☐

For Session 1

You will need attendance and membership statistics   ☐
of your church. Check the church records. If possible
use the average attendance during November because
this month is least affected by weather and festivals.
Provide the best you can and 'guestimate' if you have
to!

For Session 2

You will need to know the numbers of church   ☐
members gained and lost over the past three years in
the categories described. Once again do the best you
can!

For Session 5

You will need to provide local maps for each   ☐
member of the group, if possible.

Very important: You will need to read through each session carefully to make sure you are well prepared and have all you need to lead the group.

Now read 'Where to Next?' on page 73.

Session 1 How Churches Grow

Growth Objective

By the end of this session you should be able to describe four dimensions of church growth and illustrate in which dimensions, if any, your church is growing.

Begin with Prayer

'But if any of you lacks wisdom, he should ask God, who gives generously to all without finding fault, and it will be given to him.' (James 1:5, NIV)

Bible Reading

Ask someone to read to the group the end of the Apostle Peter's sermon and the account of the conversion of the first Christians from Acts 2:38–47. It is a familiar passage that describes what has been called 'the birthday of the Church'. Even at this early stage in the life and growth of the Church it is possible to identify a number of different ways in which a local church can grow.

Group Discussion: How Do Churches Grow?

Briefly study and search through this passage of Scripture. If you are in a large group form buzz groups of about four people and see how many ways of growth you can discover. Ransack the passage and write what you find in the box following.

_____

_____

_____

_____

_____

_____

Leader's Time: The Four Dimensions of Growth

Note: Bring the whole group together to share their discoveries. Write the various ways of growth down on a blackboard, flipchart or overhead projector as people suggest them. Don't duplicate, but allow for variety of expression. Now introduce the four dimensions of growth.

The exercise we have just been through has been done by many others, and there have been numerous attempts to classify the various ways in which churches grow.

One of the most common caricatures of Church Growth principles is that they are only concerned with numbers. This is obviously absurd, because even the earliest research into how churches grow recognised that growth is multidimensional and involves growth in quality as well as quantity.

A very helpful analysis of church growth has been suggested by Dr Orlando Costas, a missionary scholar from Latin America. He argues that the growth of a church should be seen as 'holistic expansion' so that growth is sought in every way. In his book *The Church and Its Mission* (p. 89) he writes,

> In order for church growth to be holistic expansion it must encompass four major areas: the numerical, organic, conceptual and incarnational.

If we follow this analysis of Dr Costas, but simplify his terms, we may describe his four dimensions of growth as:

1 Growing up to maturity – conceptual growth
2 Growing together in community – organic growth
3 Growing out in service and evangelism – incarnational growth
4 Growing more in numbers – numerical growth

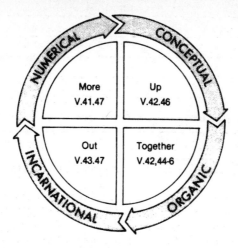

Figure 1: The Four Dimensions of Growth – Acts 2.41–7

These four dimensions of growth may be found in the Acts 2:38–47 passage, and many other passages of Scripture may be used to illustrate them. You may want to refer to those listed or introduce others during your discussions.

1 Growing Up To Maturity

In Acts 2:42,46, the first Christians began to grow to maturity by studying the Apostles' teaching and by praying and worshipping regularly. They grew in their understanding of the basic beliefs and practices of the Christian faith.

The Apostles continued to show great concern for the spiritual development and maturity of their converts and the churches they planted (Acts 8:14–17; 14:22,23; 15:36; 20:17–38; Colossians 1:28,29; I Thessalonians 2:12).

Growth to Christian maturity was brought about by knowledge of the Scriptures and by obedience to the Holy Spirit – and still is! By this dual agency of the Spirit and the Word of God, the Church as a community of faith is formed, built up and constantly renewed.

2 Growing Together in Community

Commitment to Jesus Christ embraces a commitment to the Body of Christ – the Church. Those who share the same confession that 'Jesus is Lord' come together to form the local community of faith.

In Acts 2:42, 44–46 there is great stress upon the fellowship or sharing of these first Christians. They not only shared their faith and experience, but they shared their property and possessions as well (see also Acts 4:32–5:11). Obviously their devotion to Christ and to each other knew no bounds.

This demonstration of deep Christian love and commitment to one another is extremely challenging, especially today when the practice of communal living has been relegated to particular, and sometimes peculiar, Christian groups. In the light of this experience of the Early Church in Acts, and indeed throughout the New Testament, we are forced to face a number of questions about the quality of relationships and stewardship in the contemporary Church.

Group Discussion: How Is Our Church Growing? (I)

Turn to your composite list of ways of growth discovered from Acts 2:38–47 (page 6). As a group, identify those ways that fall into the categories of Growing Up and Growing Together. Underline or ring them on your blackboard, flipchart or overhead projector.

In your group or buzz groups answer the following question: In what ways has our church been growing up and together in the past few years? Try to give specific examples to illustrate the growth (or decline), such as: 'We now have six groups meeting in homes to study the Bible and pray together every week.' 'We have formed a group of pastoral visitors who call on the sick and housebound members of the church.' 'We were not able to avoid a split two years ago between people who had very strong views about how worship should be conducted.' etc.

Leader's Time

Note: Bring the whole group together and introduce the next two dimensions.

3 Growing Out in Service and Evangelism

In Acts 2:43,47 the impact upon Jerusalem by the Church was significant. Outsiders were filled with awe, and initially with good will. As these first Christians went out to teach and preach and heal in the power of the Holy Spirit, they were conscious that the Lord Jesus was working with them and through them (Acts 3:16; 4:8–10; see also Mark 16:20). The Church's ministry is modelled on her Lord's, which was summarised in Matthew's Gospel in the following terms:

> Jesus went all over Galilee, teaching in the synagogues, preaching the Good News about the Kingdom, and healing people who had all kinds of disease and sickness. (Matthew 4:23)

The rest of the Acts of the Apostles is an account of how the ministry of Jesus in the power of the Holy Spirit continued through the Church (Acts 1:1; 9:5; 16:6,7, etc.). Throughout the history of the Church, with varying emphasis and effect, teaching, preaching and healing in the name of Christ has continued.

4 Growing More in Numbers

In Acts 2:41 we read that 'about three thousand people' were added to the Church on that Day of Pentecost. The Church continued to grow numerically as individuals repented of their sins and became followers of the Lord Jesus. (Acts 2:47; 4:4; 6:7; 9:31,35; 16:5; 21:20.)

Jesus came 'to seek and to save the lost' (Luke 19:10) and sent his disciples to preach the Gospel, 'to all peoples everywhere and make them my disciples' (Matthew 28:19). God has chosen to use his people as his ambassadors with a message of reconciliation, which calls all men to repent of their sins and believe in the Lord Jesus Christ as their Saviour, thereby receiving his gift of Salvation (Luke 24:47, Romans 10:13–17; II Corinthians 5:11–21; Ephesians 2:1–10).

Those who respond to the Gospel are born again and enter the kingdom of God; they join with others to live under the reign of God (John 3:1–21; I Peter 1:22–2:10).

The followers of Christ are countable! About a hundred and twenty are found gathered together at the beginning of the book of Acts (Acts 1:15); about three thousand more were added on the Day of Pentecost (Acts 2:41); and two decades later tens of thousands of Jews had become Christians (Acts 21:20). There were many thousands of Gentiles too.

The Church has continued to grow throughout history. Despite many setbacks, especially in Europe in this century, the latest estimates of the numerical growth of the Church (in the *World Christian Encyclopaedia*) exceed 60,000 new Christians worldwide every day!

Group Discussion: How Is Our Church Growing? (II)

Turn again to your composite list of ways of growth. Underline or ring those that fall into the categories of Growing Out and Growing More. Have all the ways been categorised under the four dimensions of growth? If not, on reflection you will probably find they can be.

In your group or buzz groups answer the following question: Has our church been growing out and more in the past few years?

Try to give specific examples to illustrate the growth, such as: 'We have introduced programmes to help the unemployed and elderly in our community.' 'We ran an evangelistic coffee bar for youth in the town last summer.' 'We added sixteen new members last year.' etc.

Leader's Time: Face the Facts

Note: Bring the whole group together again and ask a selection of people (or if you have had buzz groups, a representative from each group) to give an example from the life of your church from each of the four dimensions of growth. Write them all down under each of the separate four dimensions on your blackboard, flipchart, or overhead projector. Have you been able to illustrate growth in all four dimensions? If not, do they know why?

The rest of The Growth Book is designed to help your church grow or continue to grow in all four dimensions.

Produce the figures to complete the following tables of statistics for your church. (See Session Instructions for Session 1, page 3.)

Fill in years for the past 10 years and the current year. Then fill in the tables for each year.

Current
Year

19—	19—	19—	19—	19—	19—	19—	19—	19—	19—	19—

Average adult worship attendance: (i.e. 16 years old and over). If you have more than one service in the morning or in the evening add them together.

am											
pm											

Child attendance: (15 years old and under) attending church and/or Sunday School on a typical Sunday.

Official membership: (if one exists) or communicants

Before Next Session

1 Complete the graph on page (14) from the table of statistics above. Draw graphs for each of the different tables and distinguish each one by using different colours, or lines or dots, or by means of initials at the beginning of each line (AA – Adult Attendance; CA – Child Attendance; OM – Official Membership. If you need help don't be afraid to ask.)

2 Study the graph carefully and see if you know why there are ups and downs or plateaux. Don't discuss the graph with other members of the group – you will do that in the next session – but you can discuss it with other members of your church.

3 Ask five members of your church how they became members. Did they join because their parents were members? Did they move into the area and transfer membership from another church? Were they converted through the evangelistic work of the church and became members after instruction and baptism? Don't ask them *why* they became members; all you want to know is *how*.

End with Prayer

Merciful God,
who made all men and hate nothing
   that you have made;
you desire not the death of a sinner
but rather that he should be converted and live.
Have mercy upon your ancient people the Jews,
and upon all who have not known you,
or who deny the faith of Christ crucified;
take from them all ignorance, hardness of heart,
   and contempt for your word,
and so fetch them home to your fold
that they may be made one flock under one shepherd;
through Jesus Christ our Lord.

Alternative Service Book (of the Church of England), 1980, page 558.

Session 2 Your Church's Story

> **Growth Objective**
>
> By the end of this session you should be able to tell the story of your church's growth or decline and how you have gained and lost members over the past few years.

Begin with Prayer

'Intelligent people want to learn, but stupid people are satisfied with ignorance.' (Proverbs 15:14)

Bible Reading

Numbers 1:1–3. Moses and Aaron are told by God to conduct a census of the people of God.

Group Discussion: Understanding Your Graph

In buzz groups of about four people or as one small group, briefly share your understanding of the graph you have drawn on page 14. There will be a great variety of interpretations of the causes of the ups and downs. So do not be afraid to share how you feel about this graph of your church. Remember that the points on the graph record the results of what happened much earlier and even when the graph appears as a plateau there could have been considerable gain or loss of members or attenders. The horizontal line could simply mean your church gained as many as you lost!

Continue your discussion until everyone has had an opportunity to share his or her understanding of the graph. Don't be surprised if you have different opinions and various interpretations. You will have raised so many issues that the

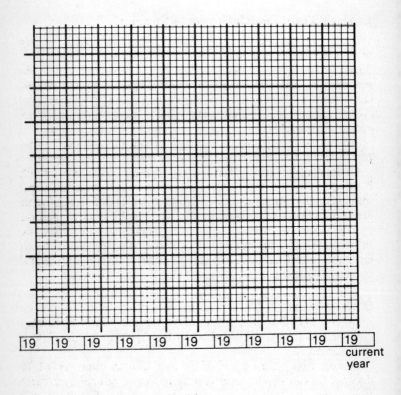

| 19 | 19 | 19 | 19 | 19 | 19 | 19 | 19 | 19 | 19 | 19 |

current
year

Plot Your Church Membership

complexity of church growth and decline will soon become obvious. You are discovering that there are no easy answers or simple solutions!

The graph should make you want to probe further. But before you can explore and then explain the causes of the growth or decline of your church, you need to understand why church growth is complex.

Leader's Time: Church Growth Is Complex

Warning: You have a lot of material to cover in this session so keep to the point and keep on the move!

Note: Bring the whole group together and ask someone to read the message to the church in Ephesus from Revelation 2:1–7. Ask someone else to read the message to the church in Smyrna from Revelation 2:8–11. Everyone should meditate briefly in silence upon these passages of Scripture.

Now introduce 'Church Growth Is Complex' (with biblical examples from the Acts of the Apostles).

Church growth and decline is complex because the local church is affected by so many factors. Some are within its control and influence, but others are not. Before a local church is able to arrest or overcome causes of decline, and start to grow or increase its rate of growth, it must understand what it can and cannot do to help itself. (A fuller discussion of the complexity of Church Growth can be found in Chapter Two of *How Do Churches Grow?* by Roy Pointer.)

Local Church Factors

(Acts 6:1–7. Priorities of ministry, organisation of leadership and pastoral care are established by the Apostles for the church at Jerusalem.)

Factors within the control of the local church cause growth or decline. Obviously the local church has most control over these factors, and we will be concentrating on many of them for the rest of this book. For example, issues such as the quality of worship or involvement in evangelism are within the control of your church.

Local Community Factors

(Acts 19:23–20:1. Pagan worship centred upon the Temple of Artemis and the scheming of Demetrius threaten the existence of the church at Ephesus.)

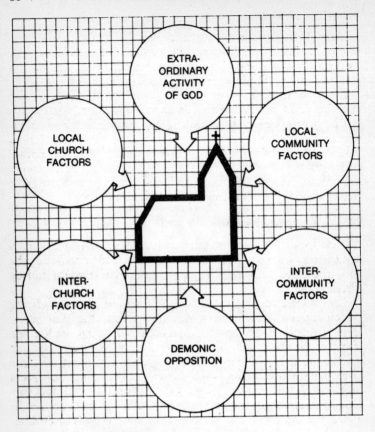

Figure 2: Church Growth is Complex

Factors in a community will often also affect the local church. Populations vary and change in size, age, race, religion, occupation and social class. Industries and companies that employ many people rise and fall. Attitudes to God and the Church also vary from place to place. All these factors in a community will affect the local church for good or ill.

Inter-Church Factors

(Acts 15:1–35. The decision of the Council of Jerusalem favours Gentile evangelisation. The missionary-minded church of Antioch rejoices at the prospect of increased church growth and planting among the Gentiles of the Roman Empire and beyond.)

Every local church has formal or informal contacts with churches and Christians within its own denomination and outside in the wider Christian fellowship. Denominational or inter-church decisions or emphases may greatly affect the local church. But of course churches *do* have some control: they can choose either to bar or embrace doctrines, hymns, programmes or preachers. However, if a bishop refuses to replace a curate there is little the local parish church or incumbent can do.

Inter-Community Factors

(Acts 13:4ff. The great missionary journeys of the Apostle Paul and the easy travels of other Christians were made possible by the good roads and safe sea voyages of the Roman communications system.)

The social, ideological and technological factors of the surroundings affect a local church. A church in the black townships of South Africa has different factors affecting its life and ministry than a church in suburban Surrey. A church planted among the tribes of Papua New Guinea is not faced with the same materialistic media bombardment as the affluent churches of North America. Over these sorts of factors, local churches have little direct control, but it is important for the church to be aware of them and their possible effect upon growth or decline.

Demonic Opposition

(Acts 16:16–18. The confrontation with the slave-girl who had an evil spirit at Philippi was a rejection of demonic testimony by Paul. He, like Jesus, would tolerate no compromise with the Devil and permit no confusion in the proclamation of the Gospel.)

The Devil and demonic forces constantly wage war against the kingdom of God and the growth of the Church. Whether evil is entrenched in the structures of society or the hearts and minds of men and women, the battle against demonic opposition rages on. The local church must be consistently on its guard and on the offensive. If you cannot identify three causes of decline or three of growth, write down just one or two.

Extraordinary Activity of God

(Acts 8:4–25. The conversion of very many Samaritans through the preaching of Philip is clear biblical evidence of a 'tribe' or people group turning to Christ in large numbers and at the same time. Similar examples have been seen throughout Church history.)

By 'extraordinary' we mean those movements or 'visitations' of the Holy Spirit in revival and 'People Movements' that bring large numbers of people to Christ. A church in the midst of such movements will grow very rapidly. Its primary responsibility at such times is to remain open to the direction of the Holy Spirit and to preserve and care for the flood of converts.

Finally . . .

Note: Ask someone to read the message to the church at Thyatira from Revelation 2:18–29. Ask someone else to read the message to the church at Laodicea from Revelation 3:14–22. Listen carefully to these readings and note how factors from inside and outside affected the churches. As you listen, see if you can identify the factors we have mentioned in this session. Church growth was as complex in the first century as it is in the twentieth.

Group Discussion: Are We Responsible?

Return to your group or buzz groups to answer the following question: Has the decline or growth of our church been affected by factors within our control? What are they? Briefly discuss your answer to this question and then reassemble as a whole group.

Leader's Time

Note: Ask each group (or if you are a small group, each person) to share what factors within your church's control they believe to have caused decline. List them on a blackboard, flipchart or overhead projector. When you have written down all the suggestions, ask the group to identify the three most serious causes of decline, or hindrances to growth.

Write them in the box following. Now, repeat the exercise for causes of growth. We will return to these later.

Cause of decline or hindrance to growth
1
2
3
Cause of growth
1
2
3

Group Discussion: How Members Join our Church

Return to your small group or buzz group. Share what you discovered between sessions about how five people in church became members. When everyone has shared you will have learned a great deal about how your church has gained its members.

Leader's Time: How Members Are Gained and Lost

Understanding and analysing how members are gained and lost is one of the most important exercises a church can do. Far too many churches are keen and eager to see people joining but seldom notice or care when they leave.

Members are gained in four ways:

1 Biological Growth

This takes place when the children of committed Christian parents come to faith and join the church. Perhaps the children, when of responsible age, are confirmed or baptised as believers; or they put on a Salvation Army uniform; or they submit to some other initiation rite that recognises them as responsible church members.

2 Transfer Growth

This takes place when committed Christians move from one church and become members of another, either locally or distant: one church gains at the other church's expense.

3   Restoration Growth

This takes place when lapsed Christians who have failed to worship or practise their faith regularly for (say) at least two years are restored to active Christian commitment and church membership.

4   Conversion Growth

This takes place when people with no Christian history or experience are brought to repentance and faith, accept Jesus Christ as Saviour and Lord, and join a local church as responsible church members.

Members are lost in three ways:

1   By Death

Church members die and they join the roll of the Church Triumphant!

2   By Transfer

Church members transfer their membership to other churches because of removal to another area or disaffection with a local church.

3   By Reversion

Church members lapse and cease to gather for worship and maintain Christian practice on a regular basis. Using figure 3, fill in the numbers of people in the various categories for the past three years. (The leader will provide the actual figures or best estimates: see Session Instructions for Session 2, page 3.)

Group Discussion: The Value of Categories

In your small group or buzz groups discuss the value of these categories for describing the gains and losses of church members or attenders, and the significance of the grand totals for the past three years. The following notes may prove helpful.

1   The amount of biological growth indicates the effectiveness of your Sunday School and Youth programmes. It also reflects the quality of Christian education provided in the home. Sadly, of course, not all the children of committed Christians follow the

	Biological growth	Transfer growth	Restoration growth	Conversion growth	Total annual gain		Loss by death	Transfer out	Reversion	Total annual loss
19—										
19—										
19—										
Grand totals										

Figure 3

faith of their parents. Our survey suggests two-thirds do. (See 'What Are Churchgoers Like?': MARC Monograph no 6.) If we are seeing only a few of our children or young people following Christ and joining the church, then we have to ask some probing questions about the validity of the Christian instruction we are giving them both at home and in the church.

2   The amount of Transfer Growth reflects the warmth of welcome and quality of worship when visitors come to your church. First impressions are all-important. You are not out to 'sheep-steal', but for some people one church is more acceptable than another. Ideally Transfer Growth will come through Christians moving into your neighbourhood who will join your church rather than another. Beware, however, of thinking that new members are new Christians. They were already Christians when they came, and are not new converts.

3   Adding members by Restoration Growth is a particularly difficult but very rewarding task. Careful counsel and loving fellowship for lapsed Christians are vitally important, as is a programme to try to help them back.

4   Conversion Growth is the fruit of effective evangelism, that is committed to 'making disciples' and caring for new Christians until they are active members of the church. Most churches are not very good at it!

5   Loss by Transfer is a serious problem in churches where the local population is highly mobile and constantly moving on. If, however, members are constantly transferring to other local chur-

ches perhaps relationships are not what they ought to be or their other needs are not being met.

6   Loss by Reversion needs particular study. Failure in Christian education or care are common causes. Sometimes new members find it difficult to join church groups and activities; they quickly become disillusioned and feel rejected. If your church is constantly losing members by Reversion you must quickly plug the gap.

Leader's time

Summarise: In this session we have moved on from recognising the need for our church to grow in all four dimensions and have focused particularly upon the numerical growth or decline of our church.

The graph has given us some clues about the causes of numerical growth and decline and the study of the gains and losses has helped us focus on some specific issues. Do we want to share some of our discoveries at other church meetings and groups, e.g. with Sunday School teachers, the Church Council, House Group leaders, etc.? If so, then we need prayerfully to decide how. Begin to pray about this in preparation for our follow-up to our study of *The Growth Book*.

Before Next Session

In the next session we will examine the health of our church. In order to prepare please read and meditate upon Ephesians 4:1–16. Be prepared to answer the following questions: 'What does it mean for Jesus Christ to be the Head of our Church?' and 'What changes, if any, are required to put Jesus Christ in control of every part of our church?'

End with Prayer

'So the churches were strengthened in the faith and grew daily in numbers.' (Acts 16:5, NIV)

Session 3 The Ideal Church

Growth Objective

By the end of this session you should be able to identify
the 'signs of growth' that are strong or weak in your church.

Begin with Prayer

'If you have ears, then, listen to what the Spirit says to the
churches. (Revelation 2:7)

Bible Reading

Ephesians 4:1–16. The building of the body of Christ.

Leader's Time: The Church of Your Dreams

How many models or pictures of the Church do you think we
could find in the New Testament? In 1961 Dr Paul S Minear
published *Images of the Church in the New Testament* in which he
identified 96 such 'images' or models. He discovered that many
different words or phrases like 'flock', 'vineyard', 'the body of
Christ', 'royal priesthood', 'a holy nation' and 'the people of God'
are used to describe the Church. He also suggests that many
churches use only one or two of these images to create what they
believe to be their ideal church, modelled on the New Testament.

Do you know how many different denominations there are in
the World Church? Dr David Barrett, editor of the *World Christian Encyclopaedia*, estimates that there were 22,190 in 1985, and
they are increasing at the rate of 270 every week!

With so many models of the church to choose from, both in

the New Testament and in the World Church today, the church of your dreams is probably very different from the dreams of someone else.

Group Discussion: Our Dream Church

As one group or in buzz groups take a few minutes to decide the following: 'If our church were perfect and the church of our dreams, it would be characterised by . . .'

Remember that you are talking about the church as people, not the building, so you are more concerned with right attitudes, belief and behaviour than with architecture and decor. As you discuss the essential features of your dream church, write the three most important ones in the box below.

In my dream church there is . . .

1 —————————————————————————

2 —————————————————————————

3 —————————————————————————

Before you move on! Since last week you have been meditating on the theme of Jesus Christ as the Head of your church. Do you believe that the three essential features you have listed above are the most important ones for Jesus? Discuss briefly and change your list if necessary.

Leader's Time: Signs of Growth

Chapter Three of *How Do Churches Grow?* describes ten 'signs of growth' that he believes characterise churches which seek to live under the Headship of Jesus Christ. The local church has been described as an outpost of the Kingdom of God, a community of believers over whom Jesus Christ reigns as king. When he does, these are 'signs' of his reign.

That book endeavours to establish the biblical foundation for the ten 'signs'. The list is not exhaustive because it recognises that there are undoubtedly other evidences of growth. However, these 'signs' were manifested in the local churches of the New Testament; they have reappeared throughout Church history during periods of renewal and awakening, and they are to be found in the growing churches of the world today.

Do we want our church to grow? If so, we can go through the list of signs as a 'Church Growth check-up'. If we discover areas of weakness, then we must actively seek to correct them. We will also be able to build upon any areas of strength we discover.

The following questionnaire is an Appendix from *How Do Churches Grow?* It is designed to help us evaluate our church by the ten 'signs of growth'. This is a subjective exercise which will give us each person's assessment of the strength or weakness of a particular sign in our church. We will add the individual scores together in the group or each buzz group. The collective total and evaluation will provide us with the basis for discussion and future action.

Group Discussion: Signs of Growth in Our Church

Within your group but as an *individual* on your own, fill in the first section of the questionnaire. Complete signs 1–5 before discussion in your group or buzz group. You will have to make some difficult decisions as you circle each number to score high or low. The lowest number is the weakest. Please be as honest as you can and don't be afraid to decide. There is no middle number so you cannot sit on the fence! When you have indicated a score for every statement about your church under each sign, add the three scores together to give a total score for the sign. Do all this by yourself. You will share the total score with your group later.

Remember that the purpose of this exercise is to examine your church in the light of the New Testament and under the guidance of the Holy Spirit. Pray, therefore, before you begin, and don't be afraid to ask for help if you have difficulty with the exercise or are not sure what to do.

Sign 1   Constant Prayer

**Please circle number
according to weakness or strength**

1   Our church has
well-attended prayer
meetings, either in homes
or at the church, every
week.

weak   1   2   3   4   strong

2   Individual and
personal prayer is
encouraged and topics
for prayer are regularly
given to church
members.

weak   1   2   3   4   strong

3   Prayer for our
community and world
needs features
prominently in the life
of our church.

weak   1   2   3   4   strong

Total score for Sign 1

Sign 2   Respect for Biblical Authority

4   When questions arise
in our church about the
Christian life or our
church activities we turn
to the Bible for
guidance.

weak   1   2   3   4   strong

5   The preaching and
teaching in our church is
based on the Bible and
related to life today.

weak   1   2   3   4   strong

6   The Bible constantly
challenges our church
about the way we behave
and what we believe.

weak   1   2   3   4   strong

Total score for Sign 2

Sign 3   *Effective Leadership*

7 Our minister/pastor/   weak   1   2   3   4   strong
priest is a person with
vision for growth and
always reminds us of the
need to reach out to
others.

8 The leaders in our   weak   1   2   3   4   strong
church are caring and
loving and are helpful in
times of trouble.

9 Our leaders know   weak   1   2   3   4   strong
where they are going
and get things done.

Total score for Sign 3

Sign 4   *Mobilised Membership*

10 Every member of   weak   1   2   3   4   strong
our church is
encouraged to discover
and use their gifts and
talents.

11 Our church   weak   1   2   3   4   strong
recognises the great
variety of spiritual gifts,
some extraordinary and
others not, and we are
willing to recognise and
accept each other's gifts.

12 We accept the truth   weak   1   2   3   4   strong
that all members have
something to contribute
to build up the body of
Christ and we are trying
to put it into practice.

Total score for Sign 4

Sign 5 Eventful Worship

13 Our worship
services are always
helpful and uplifting
times.

weak 1 2 3 4 strong

14 Everybody sings
enthusiastically and
appears joyful during
our worship.

weak 1 2 3 4 strong

15 Someone who has
never been to church
before would understand
what to do and what was
being sung or said in our
worship.

weak 1 2 3 4 strong

Total score for Sign 5

Group Discussion

Join with the rest of your group or buzz group to discover your
group score. The maximum you personally can score for any one
sign is 12 and the minimum is 3. When you have circled each
item and added up the score for each sign, share your scores with
your group. Appoint a scorer to add up the total scores for the
whole group, for each sign. Fill in your group scores in the chart
on pages 31–32.

Repeat the exercise as an individual to complete the questionnaire for signs 6–10.

Sign 6 Continuous Evangelism

Please circle number
according to weakness or strength

16 Most of our church members love Jesus Christ so much they cannot help talking about him to their relatives, friends and neighbours.   weak 1 2 3 4 strong

17 Our church has an all-year evangelistic programme of visitation, missions, guest services, etc.   weak 1 2 3 4 strong

18 New converts are regularly welcomed into our church and receive basic Christian instruction in special classes or groups.   weak 1 2 3 4 strong

Total score for Sign 6

Sign 7 Community Life

19 Our church is known for its warm, friendly and caring fellowship.   weak 1 2 3 4 strong

20 People easily feel 'at home' in our church.   weak 1 2 3 4 strong

21 Church members mix freely and regularly get together on other occasions than Sunday services.   weak 1 2 3 4 strong

Total score for Sign 7

Sign 8   Compassionate Service

22   We are always   weak   1   2   3   4   strong
looking for ways to show
God's love in our
community.

23   A number of people   weak   1   2   3   4   strong
now come to our church
because of the practical
help and care we showed
them in the past.

24   We have a number   weak   1   2   3   4   strong
of caring and helpful
activities on our
premises that are open
to all and in which
church members are
active.

Total score for Sign 8

Sign 9   Openness to Change

25   There are many   weak   1   2   3   4   strong
testimonies to changed
lives in our church.

26   We have seen many   weak   1   2   3   4   strong
changes in our church in
the past few years and
they have been accepted
without bad feelings and
divisions.

27   Our church is   weak   1   2   3   4   strong
willing to change the
way we do things if it
will help outsiders come
to know Jesus Christ.

Total score for Sign 9

Sign 10   Released Resources

28 People in our church generously give their time as well as their money for God's work.	weak	1	2	3	4	strong
29 At least 10% of our church's income is given to missions at home and overseas.	weak	1	2	3	4	strong
30 The financial giving in our church has more than kept pace with inflation.	weak	1	2	3	4	strong

Total score for Sign 10

Group Discussion

When you have completed scoring signs 6–10, share with the whole group or buzz group and fill in the group score to complete the chart below.

Leader's Note: If you have several groups meeting together you may want to add all the group scores together to obtain a grand total from all attenders.

Group Scores for Signs of Growth

Group Score

Sign 1   Constant Prayer

Sign 2   Respect for Biblical Authority

Sign 3   Effective Leadership

Sign 4   Mobilised Membership

Sign 5   Eventful Worship   ⬜

Sign 6   Continuous Evangelism   ⬜

Sign 7   Community Life   ⬜

Sign 8   Compassionate Service   ⬜

Sign 9   Openness to Change   ⬜

Sign 10 Released Resources   ⬜

Leader's Time: Where Are We Weakest?

We are now going to look at the group scores to identify those signs which have the lowest scores. They have been revealed as the weakest and have exposed areas of our church's life where action needs to be taken to rectify the situation and, with the Holy Spirit's help, bring about growth. Hopefully the changes required by Jesus Christ, the Head of our church, are being identified!

Note: Write down on a flipchart, blackboard or overhead projector the three areas that have been revealed as those of greatest weakness. Ask everyone present to write them in the appropriate column of the box below.

Area of weakness	Score (lowest at the top)	Proposed solution
1		
2		
3		

Have everyone suggest any possible solutions to correct these weaknesses. Discuss the suggestions until the group reaches general agreement and write down a brief summary of the proposed solution in the space provided. You may want to share these solutions with other church leaders and groups if appropriate. However, these proposals may need to be modified in the light of further study and understanding so don't allow the group to be too firm or dogmatic about their opinions at this stage. And remember you have learned that church growth is complex!

Before Next Session

1 If you had to convince another church member of the value of Church Growth analysis what would you say?

Write two of the positive statements you would make below:

_____

_____

_____

_____

2 Do you think the causes of decline and growth you listed on page 19 are still valid? If you want to add others, do so below.

Causes of decline	Causes of growth
1	1
2	2
3	3

End with Prayer

Thank God for the signs of growth that have been revealed as strong in your church. Pray about the proposed solutions to areas of weakness.

Restore O Lord
In all the earth your fame
And in our time revive
The Church that bears your name
And in your anger
Lord remember mercy
Oh Living God
Whose mercy shall outlast the years.

Graham Kendrick 1981

Session 4 Analysis Paralysis

> ### Growth Objective
> By the end of this session you should know how to use Church Growth surveys and their value and limitations.

Begin with Prayer

'Let us examine our ways and test them, and let us return to the Lord.' (Lamentations 3:40)

Bible Reading

Nehemiah 2:11–18. The story of Nehemiah rebuilding the demolished city walls of Jerusalem in the fifth century BC.

Leader's Time: Facing Facts

Note: Ask people to share their positive statements from page 33 about Church Growth analysis. Write them down on a flipchart, blackboard or overhead projector. Try not to duplicate statements but compile a list representing all the positive things your group has said. You should end up with a list of the benefits and value of Church Growth surveys.

The account of Nehemiah's secret inspection of the broken down walls of Jerusalem reveals the importance of thorough examination and careful planning before repair and restoration is possible. The account has much to teach us and is a good biblical example of the need for analysis prior to action! Our Church Growth analysis is following Nehemiah's good example.

In daily affairs we are familiar with the need for regular examination and servicing to maintain domestic appliances and vehicles.

Anyone buying a house needs it surveyed in case of rising damp or dry rot. All of us recognise the value of a regular check-up by the doctor or dentist. Our church needs a check-up too.

The local church needs to be surveyed and 'serviced' if it is to maintain its spiritual vitality and true purpose. The studies in *The Growth Book* are providing tools for this purpose. We hope we can use the studies to detect a number of areas in our church where we need to repair or restore.

At this half-way point it is important that we clarify just what we have learned about the growth and decline of our church.

Group Discussion: What Have We Discovered?

In groups or buzz groups, use the insights gained from Sessions 1–3 and your list of causes of decline and growth on pages 19 and 33, to discuss briefly what you consider to be the most important facts you have discovered about the growth and decline of your church. Write them down so that you remember them.

1 _____

2 _____

3 _____

4 _____

5 _____

Leader's Time: Are Surveys Sinful?

Church Growth analysis has been criticised for being unspiritual and unbiblical. It is considered unspiritual because it allegedly ignores or undervalues the role of the Holy Spirit (John 3:8 and I Corinthians 3:6 are often cited). It is considered unbiblical because David carried out a census of Israel (I Chronicles 21:1–3) and was condemned for it. While the concerns expressed in these criticisms should be recognised, they become invalid when the motives for Church Growth analysis are pure and right. In David's case they were not!

In Numbers 1:1–3 Moses and Aaron were actually commanded to undertake a census. They were given precise instructions on how to carry out the survey, organise the people of Israel and get them prepared for God's mission. This provides us with a legitimate and indeed the primary motive for all Church Growth analysis: *to make the people of God more effective in the mission of God.*

The proper use of the surveys and analysis provided in this book will help our church to pray, live and serve even more closely to the will and purpose of God. Rather than ignore the role of the Holy Spirit we should pray that the surveys and discussions that follow will open our church to Spirit-directed change. By facing facts in our church, we should emerge from the fog that blinds so many Christians to their true situations and prevents them from realising their full potential for God. All the analysis undertaken so far should help to make our church more effective in the mission of God.

If Christians fail to act on what they have learned, either because they have more information than they need or because they do not use the information gained, then 'Analysis Paralysis' has set in. It is a common and wasteful disease and one best avoided.

How to Avoid Analysis Paralysis

Prevention is better than cure, so we must avoid 'Analysis Paralysis' by adopting the right attitude to Church Growth surveys and evaluation.

1 Undertake surveys prayerfully.
Key question: Have we asked God for understanding?
   All the data-gathering, graph interpretation and church evaluation we have done and will do, must be undertaken in a prayerful attitude of dependence upon God. Measurement of effectiveness in God's mission requires the discernment of his will and purpose for our church. What does God want us to do? What does he want us to be like?

2 Face facts honestly.
Key question: Are there any facts we are not prepared to face?
   Fact-facing is often a painful process and the temptation is to avoid the difficult and disturbing truth, especially about ourselves and our churches. However, once we are prepared to accept the facts as a foundation upon which to build, they become the first step to good planning for improvement. Facing facts honestly helps us to become better stewards of God's resources both in our own lives and in our churches.

3 Use research specifically.
Key question: How does this information help us make disciples?

No one needs to know everything about their church. However, if we want to grow we need to know the essential facts about matters that help and hinder growth, especially numerical increase through making disciples. Therefore analysis needs to be focused on areas of church life that affect our obedience as a church to the Great Commission.

4 Apply discoveries correctively.
Key question: Are we using what we have learned to improve our performance?

Church Growth surveys should provide information that can be used to correct the failings and faults discovered, so that weaknesses may be overcome and strengths enhanced. Having diagnosed the illness the surveys should help us to prescribe the remedy quickly.

5 Act on findings practically.
Key question: What should we do now?

What has been discovered must be acted upon, as resources allow. We must take account of the people in our church, their gifts or talents, our church finances and buildings, etc. Then we can decide upon what action we must take now.

Group Discussion: Going for Growth

In your group or buzz groups take one of the areas of weakness listed on page 32. You may have decided, for example, that you are not a 'praying church'. You realise that prayer is limited or apparently non-existent in the life of your church. Now follow the sequence listed under 'How to avoid Analysis Paralysis' and ask all the 'key questions' of your chosen 'discovery'.

For example:

1 Have we asked God for understanding of the reason for the lack of prayer in our church?
2 Are there any facts about our lack of prayer we are not prepared to face?
3 How does our lack of prayer affect the making of disciples?
4 What have we discovered that could help us improve the prayer life of our church?
5 What should we do now about prayer in our church?

Express your answer to Question 5 as a Growth Goal.

For example: 'We are going to start four meetings in church members' homes for prayer and Bible study.' 'We will invite people to come early to worship for a time of prayer before the service begins.'

Now complete the exercise for as many of the 'discoveries' listed on pages 33 and 36 as time allows, or the 'discoveries' require.

Be sure to write down your Growth Goals, as we will return to them in the final session.

Growth Goal 1

_____

Growth Goal 2

_____

Growth Goal 3

_____

Growth Goal 4

_____

Growth Goal 5

Before Next Session

1   Complete the list of Growth Goals if you did not have time for them in your group.

2   Think about all the things you do personally in your church. Ask yourself the following questions:
   Why do I do them?
   Do I feel able to do them well?
   Do other church members express satisfaction with what I do in the church?
   Do I feel I am a 'square peg in a round hole'?

3   Read the following passages of Scripture:
   Romans 12.1–8
   I Corinthians 12:1–11
   Ephesians 4:7–16

4   If your church has a minister, appoint a representative from your group to ask him or her how many different things he or she does each week. If there is no objection, ask how many hours

are spent on each. If your church doesn't have a minister or other similar leader, then pretend that you do and use the list of activities on pages 42–43 to plan his week. You will soon realise just how busy, and often too busy, ministers are.

End with Prayer

Pray for each member of your group. Thank God for the good qualities and characteristics of each member. If you are able to, express your thankfulness openly to members within the group.

Session 5 Ban One-man Bands

Growth Objective

By the end of this session you should know how to discover your spiritual gifts and the gifts of others.

Begin with Prayer

'Each one should use whatever gift he has received to serve others, faithfully administering God's grace in its various forms.' (I Peter 4:10, NIV)

Bible Reading

Romans 12:1–8. The body of Christ functions as each member uses his different gifts according to the grace and power God has given him.

Group Discussion: Who Works Only on Sunday?

In your group or buzz group decide how many hours per week your minister (or other church leaders if you do not have one, or an imaginary minister!) spends on each of the following activities. The list is a typical one and you may have been given some specific information from your minister or church leader during the past week. He or she may even be a member of your group! Complete the exercise as an *individual* before sharing with your group for discussion.

Number of
hours per
week

1   Pastoral visiting – time spent with church
members and other people in the parish or
community in their homes, in hospital, in prison,
etc.

2   Prayer and Bible Study – devotional time
spent in praying for people and circumstances
in the church and community and studying God's
Word.

3   Sermon Preparation – time spent in preparing
for sermons and addresses given at worship
services and on other public occasions.

4   Preaching and Teaching – time spent in actual
preaching or teaching at worship services and
during classes or meetings for new members,
Bible Study, Sunday School teachers, Small
Group leaders, etc.

5   Church Administration – time spent on
general church administration, correspondence,
telephoning, church council and business
meetings, etc.

6   Counselling – time spent counselling
individuals with personal and spiritual
problems, couples preparing for marriage, the
bereaved, requests for baptism, etc.

7   Evangelism – time spent engaged in, and
training others in, the sharing of the Good News
by calling on people who never attend church or
at specially planned evangelistic events.

8   Denominational and interdenominational
responsibilities – time spent in Synod,
Association, District or Provincial council
meetings and affairs. Also, time spent at inter-
church committees, meetings or events.

9 Community Leadership – time spent in
   community roles as chaplain, school
   governor, attendance at public meetings, etc.

10 Family and relaxation – time spent resting.

11 Planning – time for strategic thinking ahead.

Now add the total number of hours per week

How many hours have you suggested the minister or church
leader works each week? One person's total in a similar exercise
exceeded 200 hours! Share your total with the other members of
the group. Discuss the differences briefly.

People today, and a minister or church leader is no exception,
need time for their families, for leisure, home maintenance, etc,
and they work about 40 hours a week. Obviously, if a minister
is to attempt to do all the activities listed above (and remember
they are only a selection), he will have to set some priorities and
receive help by sharing ministry with others.

This exercise should show very clearly that church leaders
cannot possibly do everything, no matter how well they are gifted
and trained. They need to see their role in the light of Ephesians
4:11,12 as 'equippers' or 'enablers', whose task is to 'prepare all
God's people for the work of Christian service, in order to build
up the body of Christ.'

Leader's Time: 'All Of You Are Christ's Body' (Corinthians 12:27)

We have now identified one of the great problems of the modern
church – 'clericalism', the domination of the church by the clergy.
The minister, either by choice or custom, has become the sole
'professional' Christian, who alone is equipped and authorised
to exercise Christian ministry. In churches suffering from this
problem the pastor or priest is paid to do all the work of the
church and the members are merely passive spectators or
listeners. Whenever this type of minister thinks of involving the
lay people his first thought – so a recent survey revealed – is
likely to be for people to clean the church!

Nothing could be further from the Church of the New Testament than this contemporary caricature of the body of Christ. It has often been said that many a modern church has become a grotesquely deformed body consisting of a 'mouth and bottom'.

Church Growth studies from every part of the world have universally demonstrated that the mobilisation of the laity is a major factor contributing to the growth of churches. The key to mobilising all the people of God is a proper understanding of spiritual gifts – the recognition that all God's people have been gifted by the Holy Spirit to exercise a great variety of spiritual ministries.

Dr C Peter Wagner writing on this subject in his book, *Your Church Can Grow* (p 73) says:

> In the light of the doctrine of spiritual gifts, mobilisation of church members for growth – or any spiritual activity – must begin with whatever process is necessary for every church member to discover his or her spiritual gift. After this the gift must be developed and put to full use through appropriate channels and structures.

But how are we to discover, develop and begin to use our spiritual gifts? Dr Wagner suggests we take five steps:

1 Explore the possibilities.
Read and study the lists of gifts in the New Testament. Know the options that appear in the Word of God so that you have something specific to look for as you move ahead.

2 Experiment with as many as possible.
If you do not try a particular gift, you will have a hard time knowing whether you have it or not. Obviously there are some gifts in the list that are hard to know how to experiment with. No one should jump off a tall building to see if he has the gift of miracles, for example. But many of them, including the gift of evangelist, lend themselves to serious experimentation.

3 Examine your feelings.
If you try a gift out and enjoy doing it, that is a good sign. On the other hand if you find yourself disliking the task the gift involves, that in itself may be a good sign that God hasn't given it to you.

4 Evaluate your effectiveness.
Spiritual gifts are functional. Each one is designed to accomplish some specific objective. If you begin to think you have a certain

spiritual gift be sure that you see the appropriate results when you use it. If you get no results, you may not have the gift.

5 *Expect confirmation from the body.*
No gifts can be discovered, developed or used alone. Why? Because they are given to members of a total organism, the body. If you have a spiritual gift, it will fit with others. Other Christians will recognise your gift and confirm to you that you have it. If you think you have a gift, but no one else agrees you have it, be very suspicious of your assessment in the matter.

Once these steps are taken and surrounded with much prayer, you should be able to answer clearly and concisely when asked: 'What is your spiritual gift?'

Group Discussion: Explore the Possibilities

This is not the place to undertake a thorough study of spiritual gifts or lead you through all five steps suggested by Dr Wagner. That will require a process of prayerful study and working out over many months, if not years. However, we can make a start by taking the first step in exploring the possibilities.

Ask someone to read Romans 12:1-8 to your group or buzz group. Using your knowledge of this passage, the two other passages you read during the week (1 Corinthians 12:1-11 and Ephesians 4:7-16) and any other relevant passages of Scripture, write down whether you think the statements are true or false in the questionnaire below. Answer the questions *individually*, on your own and without discussion, before discussing all your answers in the group.

Leader's Time: God's Different Gifts

Note: Ask someone to read aloud I Peter 4:7-12.
In this passage from I Peter we are reminded, once again, of the variety of spiritual gifts. We have read and heard of many different gifts and ministries. Some are spectacular and extraordinary, such as healing and speaking in tongues. Others appear to be rather ordinary and unspectacular, like hospitality and teaching.

In order to explore further the great variety of gifts let us examine more closely the various passages of Scripture we have referred to in this Session.

	True	False
1 Every church member has been gifted by the Holy Spirit to fulfil a particular function within the life and service of our church.	☐	☐
2 Different spiritual gifts have been given to all church members, so that only together can we function properly as a church.	☐	☐
3 Church leaders are gifted to lead and are responsible to help church members discover, develop and use their spiritual gifts.	☐	☐
4 Spiritual gifts and natural talents are not the same and priority should be given to spiritual gifts in the church.	☐	☐
5 Spiritual gifts must be exercised by all church members in the context of love, humility and faith.	☐	☐

Following your group discussion take five minutes to write down in a sentence or two what you personally have learned about spiritual gifts.

_____

_____

_____

Note: Ask your group to turn to the passages listed below and call out the gifts and ministries they can identify. Write them down on a flipchart, blackboard or overhead projector. If different versions of the Bible are used the various translations will increase understanding and certain gifts will be described in several ways. Write them all down but identify duplication of gifts where the same gift is referred

*to in different passages. For example, the gift of prophecy is referred
to several times.*

*Ask group members to copy down the lists of gifts in the appropriate
boxes below.*

Romans 12:6–8:_____

_____

_____

_____

I Corinthians 12:8–11, 28–30:_____

_____

_____

_____

Ephesians 4:7–11; I Peter 4:7–12 and any other passages: __

_____

_____

_____

Of course, all the above passages of Scripture are from the
New Testament and we also need to ask how the Holy Spirit
equipped God's people in the Old Testament. If the group has
suggestions write them down in the box below.

Examples of the Holy Spirit equipping God's people in the
Old Testament:_____

_____

_____

_____

From these lists we can see the great variety of ways in which God has gifted his people to serve him. The task for all of us now is to discover our spiritual gifts so that we may serve him too.

Before Next Session

1   Prayerfully consider how you are going to discover, develop and use your spiritual gift or gifts.

2   Obtain a local map, if your leader has been unable to provide you with one, and the latest local newspaper. Mark the parish or community boundary on the map. Read the newspaper and attempt to locate the stories and events on your map and within your boundary. Bring the map and newspaper with you to the next session.

3   Read the following passages of the 'Great Commission': Matthew 28:18–20; Mark 16:14–20; Luke 24:36–49; John 20:19–23; Acts 1:6–11. Try to memorise a part or the whole of one passage.

End with Prayer

Pray for your minister or church leader, or one that you know, especially if he or she has become burdened by the heavy load of Christian ministry. Pray that you will be shown ways to express your love and support for your minister and share the joy with him or her of serving Jesus through your church.

Take my love; my lord I pour
At Thy feet its treasure-store;
Take myself, and I will be,
Ever, only, all for Thee.

Frances Ridley Havergal, 1836–79

Session 6 Go and Make Disciples

Growth Objective

By the end of the session you should be able to test the evangelistic activity of your church and help make it more effective at making disciples.

Begin with Prayer

Jesus said, 'The Son of Man came to seek and to save the lost'. (Luke 19:10)

Bible Reading

Luke 10:1–20. Jesus trains his followers to preach the Good News of the Kingdom.

Leader's Time: Know Your Neighbour

In Acts 1:8, Jesus told his disciples, 'you will be my witnesses in Jerusalem, and in all Judea and Samaria, and to the ends of the earth.' (NIV) They had to begin to witness where they were – in Jerusalem – to the community of people who lived around them. That is where we must begin too.

If we are going to witness to our community we must get to know it well. We need to know our neighbours. So far in our studies we have been looking at ourselves. We have learned a great deal about how we are growing, or failing to grow. We know how church members have joined and left us. Many of our strengths and weaknesses have been exposed and we know we have been gifted by God to share our Christian faith and lives with others. Now it is time to look outwards, to find the people who need to know Jesus Christ as Saviour and Lord as we do.

Group Discussion: Who Is My Neighbour?

In your group or buzz group discuss your map and your attempt to relate the local newspaper to it. Share what you learned about the joys and sorrows of the people who live in your community – discover who your neighbours are.

Briefly answer and discuss the following questions. Brainstorm questions 1 and 2.

1 What kinds of people are they? Are they mostly rich or poor, young or old? Are they of different races and various religions? What kind of houses do they live in – large and luxurious, affluent apartments, urban tenements? How many have cars? How do they differ from the people in our church?

2 On the basis of our knowledge of the life and ministry of Jesus where would we expect him to be teaching, preaching and healing in our community today? (Matthew 4:23). And is our church active there in his name?

3 How does our church attempt to evangelise our community? What have we done as individuals or in our groups to share our faith with others?

Leader's Time: '3P' Evangelism

Strictly speaking, evangelism in the New Testament is the announcing of the Good News about Jesus (Acts 8:35; 17:18; I Corinthians 1:23). However, the practice of evangelism, both in the New Testament and today, embraces a host of different activities: so many activities, in fact, that the precise definition of evangelism is fraught with controversy. The Church Growth movement has sought to clarify matters by advocating effective evangelism consisting of three essential elements, the three 'Ps': *Presence*, *Proclamation*, and *Persuasion*.

Presence

This is the witness of works, that is to say good deeds or miraculous events, which provide a starting point for explaining the Gospel. These works glorify the Father and attract an inattentive world (Matthew 5:18). The witness of works is a foundation for the witness of words and a platform for proclaiming the Good News. (Acts 3:6–16; Ephesians 2:8–10).

Proclamation

This is the witness of words through the communication of the Gospel message (I Corinthians 1:21; II Timothy 1:13). This heralding of the Good News includes a call to respond in repentance and faith (Mark 1:15; Acts 2:38; 17:30). We must be concerned to get the message right and get the message across.

Persuasion

This describes that part in the process of evangelism by which those who confess Jesus Christ as Saviour and Lord are added to the church (II Corinthians 5:11). They are encouraged to repent of their sins, profess faith in God through Jesus Christ and commence Christian instruction; they are set on the way of discipleship to become responsible church members; they receive Christian initiation and are incorporated into a local church (Acts 2:42–7).

If our evangelism is to be effective it should contain all three elements. Our church should practise '3P' evangelism!

Types of Churches

Many churches and Christians are known for doing good in their communities, and rightly so, for they are following the example of their Lord (Acts 10:38). They minister to the sick, help the homeless, are concerned for the poor and promote justice and righteousness. These churches and Christians have established Presence, but they fail to Proclaim and Persuade. Let's call this type of church *Church A*.

Other churches occasionally burst into a flurry of activity to engage in Proclamation in their community. Sadly, because they have failed to build a foundation of Presence their message lacks credibility. Like Indians on a raid they take a scalp or two and run home! Let's call this type of church *Church B*.

Yet other churches establish Presence and engage in continuous Proclamation in their communities. However, they are hesitant to Persuade by calling for repentance and faith or by offering discipleship training that leads to Christian initiation. They believe this is not their business and prefer to leave it all to the Holy Spirit. They cultivate the soil and sow the seed but neglect to harvest. They forget that while the harvest is the Lord's, he has commissioned his people to bring his harvest home. Let's call a church of this type *Church C*. (Eddie Gibbs' book *Followed or Pushed*, MARC Europe: 1987, defines other types of churches, too, in a most lively and amusing way.)

Dr Donald McGavran is known as the 'father' of the Church Growth movement for his original research into church growth in India in the 1930s and his subsequent work through the School of World Mission and the Institute of Church Growth at Pasadena, California. In his book *Ten Steps for Church Growth* (p. 54) he writes:

> When Titus came back from Macedonia, he found Paul in the Corinthian synagogues arguing and 'persuading'. There is a good biblical basis for assuming that God frequently persuades through us. If we sit quietly in our corner and refuse to persuade, we are actually being disobedient to the Holy Spirit. We are refusing to follow God's leading. We should build persuasion right into our evangelism. Without persuasion, without intending for people to become disciples of Jesus Christ, evangelism is a thin anaemic substitute for the real thing. Persuasion is an essential part of effective evangelism.

Group Discussion: How Effective Is Our Evangelism?

In your group or buzz group identify the evangelistic activities that are carried out by your church under the headings Presence, Proclamation, and Persuasion.

Fill in the relevant boxes with the activities:

Presence activities: _____
_____
_____
_____

---

*Proclamation Activities:*_____

_____

_____

_____

---

*Persuasion activities:*_____

_____

_____

_____

If your boxes are not very full, don't worry. You will attempt to fill them later. If there are areas of overlap and some activities appear in more than one box, again don't worry. These activities are obviously creating more effective evangelism.

Having filled in the boxes as best you can, how would you describe your church: type A, B, or C? Or are all three elements in evangelism present? Discuss your answer and see if you can agree what type of church you are, or are most like, and how to overcome areas of weakness you have identified.

Leader's Time: Begin Where People Are

A fundamental principle in all Christian communication, following the example of Jesus, is that it should begin where people are. In the words of John: 'The Word became a human being and, full of grace and truth, lived among us. We saw his glory, the glory which he received as the Father's only Son'. (John 1:14) God condescended to become a human being through the life of Jesus: he came to where we are. Jesus became like us, although without sin, in order to communicate the Good News of the kingdom of God.

In the process of communication, by word and deed, Jesus used levels of language, illustrations and examples, parables and stories, in fact all the available teaching methods, to get his message across. He was able to communicate to all types and conditions of people. He dealt with each group or person in such a way that the seeker could see and the lost be found. In communication terms he was 'receptor-oriented' and began where people were.

The Apostles followed the example of their Lord by also beginning where people were. Peter could assume a knowledge of the Old Testament and Jewish history when he preached in Jerusalem on the Day of Pentecost (Acts 2:14–39). However, he made no such assumption when preaching in the non-Jewish home of Cornelius (Acts 10:34–43).

When Paul preached to the Jews and God-fearers of Antioch in Pisidia (Acts 13:16–41), he built upon their knowledge of God and the Old Testament. Among the animists and spirit-worshippers of Lystra he began with the concept of God as creator (Acts 14:14–18). And in Athens, among the idolatrous Greeks and their philosophers, Paul aroused their curiosity about the name and character of an unknown god (Acts 17:16–34).

As our Lord and the Apostles began where people were, surely we ought to do the same in our day. A very useful communication tool called the 'Engel Scale' (after the man who first published it) has been designed to help us in this task. It was developed to improve the use of Christian radio programmes for evangelism in Thailand. Listeners were identified as being in specific categories so that programmes could be designed to meet their needs and teach them more about Christ. The programme had to begin where people were, by attracting and holding their attention, or be switched off.

Remember that the Engel Scale is an aid to communication, or really a communicator's 'tool'. It will help you plan the most effective ways of getting the Gospel message across.

The Engel Scale has been modified and presented in various forms since originally published in *What's Gone Wrong with the Harvest?* by Engel and Norton (p. 45). The scale has obvious merits for the sensitive witness and evangelist. If you talk to someone who is interested in Christianity (−7) but unaware of the Gospel, you need to make that person aware of the basic facts of the Gospel and the implications of becoming a Christian. To call for repentance and faith (−1) when the person doesn't know what the Gospel is and what following Christ demands, would surely be extremely foolish and insensitive. Nevertheless so many Christians never stop to consider such matters and often do make

- 10	Awareness of supernatural
- 9	No effective knowledge of Christianity
- 8	Initial awareness of Christianity
- 7	Interest in Christianity
- 6	Aware of basic facts of the gospel
- 5	Grasp of implications of being a Christian
- 4	Positive attitude to becoming a Christian
- 3	Aware of personal need of salvation
- 2	Challenge and decision to turn to Christ
- 1	Repentance and faith
0	A new disciple is born
+ 1	Evaluation of decision
+ 2	Initiation into the Church
+ 3	Growing discipleship

such calls! There is not sufficient space in this book to elaborate further. Additional reading is listed on page 75.

However, even from this simple table we see various questions which may be asked of people believed to be in the different categories: questions that will enable us to communicate the Gospel more sensitively and relevantly.

Group Discussion: Begin Where My People Are

In your group or buzz group discuss your answers to the questions related to the category of people on the Engel Scale overleaf. Then use your answers and understanding to show how you propose to evangelise people you know – your friends, relatives, neighbours, workmates, etc. Try to place them on the Engel Scale and suggest an evangelistic activity that you can place in the appropriate Presence, Proclamation, Persuasion box on pages 52–53. Use a different colour pen or some means to distinguish the activities you are now suggesting from those already listed. You are beginning to improve the evangelism of your church.

Category of People

-9	How can we evangelise those who are aware of the supernatural (spiritualists perhaps); who have no effective knowledge of Christianity?
-8	In what ways can we help our workmates, who are aware of Christianity, become interested?
-6	John is aware of the basic facts of the Gospel. How can we help him grasp what it means to become a Christian?
-2	Was the evangelist right to keep calling for repentance and faith when so many people were totally unaware of the basic facts of the Gospel? What might he have done instead?
+1	What is the most appropriate way to help two new converts evaluate their decision to follow Jesus? Especially when we know they have never been to our church before?

Before Next Session

1 Give more thought and prayer to evangelising your relatives and friends. Decide how you are going to begin to evangelise them. Why not try some of the things that came up in your discussion?

2 Write down a list of meetings you do or could attend at your church or with other Christians in your community, that are attended by the following numbers of people:

Between 3 and 12 people _____

_____

_____

Between 25 and 75 people _____

_____

_____

More than 175 people   _____

                              _____

                              _____

End with Prayer

Pray for the people in your community whom you have talked about during this session. Pray that they may be effectively evangelised and become disciples of the Lord Jesus. Pray that you will be able to obey our Lord's Great Commission to 'go and make disciples'.

Session 7 Groups and Growth

Growth Objective

By the end of this session you should be able to identify the meetings of your church that help you and other members grow.

Begin with Prayer

'Day after day they met as a group in the Temple, and they had their meals together in their homes . . .' (Acts 2:46)

Bible Reading

Hebrews 10:19–25. Be concerned for one another and do not stop meeting together.

Leader's Time: Meetings Galore

Have you ever questioned the value of so many different organised meetings in our church? If so, you may be surprised to learn that a variety of meetings is actually very important for our growth as Christians: the Christian faith should not be lived in isolation, and Christians need to meet in groups of different sizes to meet specific needs related to their spiritual development. Of course, some of our church meetings may not meet these needs and therefore may not be necessary. This session should help us make sure that all our future meetings do serve their real purpose.

Sociologists have identified three basic groupings in which people relate together. In his book *Your Church Can Grow* Dr C Peter Wagner has suggested that healthy growing churches have the ability, consciously or not, to provide three groupings to help their members grow. He calls the largest group Celebration, the secondary group Congregation and the smallest group Cell. He proposes the following formula:

Celebration + Congregation + Cell = Church

A Cell group has between 3 and 12 members, a Congregation has between 25 and 175 members and a Celebration group has more than 175 members. These numbers are approximate, and the range varies considerably before the groups become unstable and cease to fulfil their different functions. Nevertheless, these numbers will help us to identify the different groups and to appreciate their value and use in our church.

Group Discussion: Groups for Growth

In your group or buzz group, share together the individual lists of meetings you have drawn up since the last session. When you have agreed how to classify the various meetings in your church, write them in the boxes below:

Meetings of Cell size – 3 to 12 people: _____

_____

_____

_____

Meetings of Congregation size – 25 to 175 people: _____

_____

_____

_____

According to the Nationwide Initiative in Evangelism survey of churches in England, 92% of English Protestant churches had less than 150 attenders at their services in 1979. Obviously, to experience Celebration-sized meetings all of these churches will have to join with others, either of the same denomination or interdenominationally. Be sure to list such meetings if they happen in your community or are attended by members of your church.

> *Meetings of Celebration size – more than 175 people:*_____
>
> _____
>
> _____
>
> _____

Leader's Time: Too Big or Too Small?

If people say, 'Our church is too big!' they are probably not talking about the actual number of church members or attenders. They are almost certainly expressing the way they feel about their church. They feel the church is impersonal and they are lost and unwanted among so many other people. The problem they are identifying is the failure of their church to provide the right groups to meet their personal and spiritual needs. So the problem is not one of size but of structure.

The largest church in the world is believed to be the Full Gospel Church in Seoul, South Korea with over 520,000 members. They are praying for 1 million members by 1990. The church was founded by their current pastor, Dr Paul Yonggi Cho in a tent in a slum area of Seoul, on 18 May 1958. From the earliest days Dr Cho has believed that only God could set the limit on how large the church would grow.

Today the Full Gospel Church is one of the most researched churches in the world and the story of its growth is told in numerous books and articles. A most remarkable feature of the church is the more than twenty thousand small groups that meet each week. Dr Cho has developed what he calls a 'web of love' throughout the church by means of these personal and caring small groups, so that all the church members feel they 'belong'. With such a structure they do not experience the problem of so many large churches, yet they are the largest of them all!

If 520,000 is not too big for a church what is too small? When Jesus declared, 'for where two or three come together in my name, there I am with them' (Matthew 18:20, NIV), he himself set the lower limit to the size of his body.

Understanding the Groups

Cell

The Cell group provides the context for personal intimacy. It is the 'family' group where relationships form and develop and where support and encouragement may be found. Jesus would have had this group experience with his disciples. Essential activities within these small groups include open sharing of struggles and triumphs in Christian experience, life-related study of the Bible, continuous encouragement to grow to spiritual maturity and constant prayer for one another.

Of course small groups can be used for evangelism and small numbers of people meet to do other things, such as Parish Church Councils, planning meetings, etc. However, these other meetings will never compensate for the Cell group meetings: the church that fails to provide them formally or encourage them informally is denying their members this vitally important 'family' fellowship.

Congregation

The Congregation group provides the context for social fellowship where a sense of common identity and purpose is communicated and felt. This is the gathering of the clan! The members of the group have a sense of belonging and it is possible to know everyone's name, and absent members are missed.

Congregation groups meet to encourage particular activities or because of a common interest. A choir of 30 members, a youth group or womens' meeting of 60, and a midweek Bible Study meeting of 40, are all Congregation groups. Jesus would have experienced this group in the synagogue at Nazareth.

Leaders of Congregations require the gifts necessary to provide some form of pastoral oversight and for the group to function. The 'fellowship circle' of this group allows for flexible and informed relationships to develop. When the group ceases its activity and disperses, small groups automatically form. The wise leader will encourage the development of Cell groups within this larger group.

Celebration

Celebration is really the gathering of the 'tribe'. This largest group provides the context for people to reaffirm their faith and practice. The primary purpose is to provide inspiration and eventful worship that builds confidence and affirms identity as God's people. Jesus would have had this type of group experience in the worship of the Temple, especially at the great festivals when hundreds of thousands of people attended.

It is not possible, nor is it necessary to know everyone in this group. The bigger the better is often true for this 'Celebration', as a crowd always attracts a crowd and very large numbers add to the impact of the event. If a local church is not big enough to provide this group experience for its members it is a good idea to join with others, particularly at the Christian festivals.

Group Discussion: Growth Groups

In your group or buzz groups turn back to your list of meetings in the boxes on pages 56–57. Select one meeting from each sized group and discuss how they can be improved to fulfil the function or purpose described above.

Write down the proposed improvements beneath each meeting below.

1   The Cell-sized meeting

Name of meeting _____

Suggested improvements_____

_____

_____

_____

2   The Congregation-sized meeting

Name of meeting _____

Suggested improvements_____

_____

_____

_____

3   The Celebration-sized meeting

Name of meeting _____

Suggested improvements_____

_____

_____

_____

Perhaps you can share your suggestions with the whole group or
church if you feel this is appropriate.

Before Next Session

1   Write down one thing you would like to see our church doing
in one year, five years and by the year AD 2000

In 1 Year_____

_____

In 5 years _____

_____

By AD 2000 _____

_____

2   Write down two 'Growth Goals' on page 67. You may select
them from page 39 or create new ones. They should arise from
what you have learned in the previous sessions and should express
a desired programme, activity or performance that you believe
will bring growth to our church. Pray about your choice and
then write these 'Growth Goals' in your own words. Write as
briefly and specifically as possible, but don't worry if it seems
vague or 'fuzzy' at this stage. Getting it written down is the most
important thing.

Some typical Growth Goals might be: 'I would like to see our
church have well-attended prayer meetings every week.' 'Our
church should appoint a full-time administrator so that the
minister has more time to exercise his pastoral gifts.' 'We should
introduce Cell groups that meet in people's homes for Bible Study

or prayer.' 'Set up a music group to improve the music and singing during worship.'

End with Prayer

Pray for the meetings you have been discussing and about suggested improvements. Pray that all those meetings will fulfil their function in the life of your church, bringing growth in membership and giving glory to God.

Session 8 Plan to Grow

Growth Objective

By the end of this session you should be able to set goals for the growth of your church and plan for their accomplishment.

Begin with Prayer

'ask the LORD to bless your plans, and you will be successful in carrying them out.' Proverbs 16:3

Bible Reading

Philippians 3:12–16. Do your best to reach God's goal for you.

Group Discussion: Growth Goals

If you have not already done so, before your group discussion, individually write your Growth Goals below (see page 64 for instructions).

My first Growth Goal for my church is _____

_____

_____

_____

My second Growth Goal for my church is _____

_____

_____

_____

_____

In your group or buzz group discuss each other's Growth Goals and agree just one for your group. Write your group's Growth Goal in the box below. All the other goals may be equally valid for your church, but for the purpose of this exercise you will be working with your own group's Growth Goal.

Our Group Growth Goal is_____

_____

_____

_____

_____

Leader's Time: Good Goals

Good goals have five important qualities.

1 *They are relevant.*
Good goals are consistent with the God-given purpose and objectives of the church. Having determined what God wants our church to do, a good goal will focus on its accomplishment. For example, an Anglican church that recognises the need to obey the Great Commission may set the goal of holding a parish mission.

2 *They are measurable.*
Good goals are also set in time and quantified so that it is known if the goal is achieved or not. For example, the church above may decide to hold a parish mission for two weeks next year, involving a team of 20 students. The use of numbers helps to 'earth' the goal.

3 *They are achievable.*
Good goals are always an expression of faith, for they relate to
future expectations, but they should be set within achievable
boundaries. If the same Anglican church adds the conversion of
the whole community to its goal, it would be most unlikely to
happen, even if revival broke out. After much prayer they could
well set an achievable 'faith projection' to 'add 10 new converts
to the church in the next year.'

4 *They are significant.*
A good goal, if achieved, will always make a significant difference
to the church. It will accomplish the agreed objective. A parish
mission that adds 10 new converts who become active church
members in a year is a significant step towards obeying the Great
Commission and represents a significant advance for the church.

5 *They are personal.*
Good goals are personally owned by the church. They have the
'ring of truth' about them and church members feel they can
pray and work to achieve them. People have something to aim
and work for.
   Goal-setting has tremendous potential for focusing the
resources of the church toward achieving God-given ends. It is
often the means of bringing a sense of direction and purpose to
a church that has lost its way or needs to get started. When goals
are achieved the results are the cause of great celebration. Even
if they are not achieved, they provide reference points for evaluation and fresh planning.

Group Discussion: Making a Good Goal

In your group or buzz groups take your group's 'Growth Goal'
and use the qualities of a good goal to improve it. Revise the
goal until it is relevant, measurable, achievable, significant and
personal (owned by all the group).
   Write your good 'Growth Goal' in the box overleaf.
   You may want to share this goal with others and even the
whole church, if appropriate.

Leader's Time: Planning for Growth

As we come to the end of this *Growth Book* we ought to have a
vision for what our church should be like in one year, five years

┌──┐
│ *A Growth Goal for our church*   │
│ _____   │
│ _____   │
│ _____   │
│ _____   │
│ _____   │
└──┘

or in AD 2000. Caring for the future of our church means planning
ahead – beginning now.

Some Christians are hesitant to plan, forgetting that God is a
planner with a plan for the Universe (Ephesians 1:5–12): God
expects his people to be actively engaged in its fulfilment (Ephesians 2:10). We and our church are part of God's plan and chosen
instruments to accomplish his purpose. Our Christian planning
is therefore an attempt to stay within the will of God.

In *How Do Churches Grow?* (by Roy Pointer, page 169) five
simple and basic planning steps are described.

1   *Face facts.*
Facing facts, even the unpleasant ones, is essential if a foundation
for good planning is to be laid. We cannot begin to plan if we
are unwilling to face the truth about our church. It is impossible
to build upon false assumptions and wishful thinking. Fact facing
is concerned to discover, 'Where are we now?' and 'How did we
get here?'

This vital first step looks at the past and the present before
moving on to consider the future. Remember Nehemiah's inspection, (Nehemiah 2:11 ff).

2   *Establish objectives.*
At this stage of planning the crucial question being answered is,
'What are we here for?' The answers provide the broad statements of purpose that need to be framed as objectives for the
church to aim for in the future. Nehemiah knew what God
wanted him to do (Nehemiah 2:12,17,18).

In 1986 an estimated 65,000 British house groups participated

in a Lenten course of Bible studies that sought to answer the
question 'What on earth is the Church for?' If every one of those
groups could state their answers in the form of objectives, then
they would provide an 'agreed agenda' for all their churches to
work and live by.

3 Set goals.
We have already noted the difference between good and bad
goals and have practised setting them. Goal-setting answers the
question, 'What do we do?' – to achieve our objectives. Good
goals also have the remarkable ability to focus faith and motivate
church members to achieve them.

Remember that you will need to identify short-term, medium-
term and long-term goals. The Walls of Jerusalem were not
rebuilt in a day and Nehemiah and the Israelites had to build
section by section over several weeks (Nehemiah 6:15). In the
same way a long-term goal will often be reached by the stone-
stepping achievements of short-term goals.

4 Make plans.
Plans are drawn up in answer to the question 'How do we achieve
our goals?' A great variety of planning techniques are available
and may easily be learned at courses and from books (see books
by David Cormack in the bibliography). Most churches have
men and women who are able managers and planners in their
day-to-day employment and could use these skills in the church.
Sadly many ministers have never had management training and
some are unwilling to make use of either the techniques or the
skills of modern managers to achieve God-given goals.

God is not glorified by the wasting of his resources or bungling
inefficiency in his work, so good planning is essential. Nehemiah's detailed planning is well documented in Nehemiah 3:1–32.

5 Assess results.
As the process of planning is an attempt to follow God's plan for
our church, we must be willing constantly to monitor its progress
by evaluation and review. If obstacles are encountered or mistakes
made they have to be overcome. Lessons will be learned and
some revision of the plan may well be required. At this stage the
crucial question is 'What is God teaching us?'

Nehemiah's assessment of the progress in building the Wall
of Jerusalem identified forces opposed to him and adjustments
required to his plan to deal with them. The account of the

practical steps he took to defend and rebuild demonstrate an amazing determination to achieve his goal! And achieve it he did (Nehemiah 6:15). Of course this great achievement was not solely due to Nehemiah's brilliant management of the Jews' strenuous efforts, as Nehemiah is quick to point out – 'everyone knew that the work had been done with God's help' (Nehemiah 6:16). When we achieve our goals, will we be able to say the same?

Group Discussion: Faith in the Future

In your group or buzz groups let all members share their vision of what they believe your church will be like in one year, five years and in the year AD 2000. Don't discuss, but simply share your vision in hope and faith about the future of your church. When you have shared these together, bring all your hopes for your church to God in prayer.

Pray about the Growth Goal your group has agreed on page 70 and pray about the planning for its achievement.

End with Prayer

Finally, commit all you have said and done in the study of this book to Jesus Christ:

To him who by means of the power working in us is able to do so much more than we can ever ask for, or ever think of: to God be the glory in the church and in Christ Jesus for all time, for ever and ever! Amen. (Ephesians 3:20,21)

Where to Next?

You Have Begun

The Growth Book has been written to help create a climate for, and raise an expectation of, growth in your church. Many areas of your church's life and witness have been discussed and reviewed and the need for change or development recognised. A host of issues have been faced and informal decisions taken in the context of the way you have studied this book. Much still needs to be done and the talking has to be acted upon. What you have completed in this course of studies is only the beginning, but at least you have begun!

Be Patient

As you try to implement the decisions taken during these studies and seek to achieve the goals you have agreed, remember that others in your church will need to pass through a similar learning experience. Be patient as you endeavour to pass on what you have discovered: this is vitally important if change is required. People need time to learn about the nature of the change and why it is necessary. They then need to be persuaded personally about the value of the change and the decision they are required to make to accept it. All of this takes time! So be loving and patient with others as you pray and work for the growth of your church. Church arguments and splits are seldom edifying and often lead to the very opposite from your desire – rather than church growth, church decline.

Be Prayerful

All church life, especially matters related to growth, must be constantly brought before God in prayer. As we have seen, prayer plays a vital part in every dimension of growth and all aspects of the Church's mission. Someone has suggested that the Church in the Acts of the Apostles 'advanced on its knees'! If we prayed as they did we might see the results they saw.

Be Persistent

You may have only begun but you are on your way. So don't give up! Remember the Great Commission will be in force until the end of time and we must endeavour to obey it:

> Go, then, to all peoples everywhere and make them my disciples: baptize them in the name of the Father, the Son, and the Holy Spirit, and teach them to obey everything I have commanded you. And I will be with you always, to the end of the age. (Matthew 28:19,20)

Further Reading

General

Barrett, David (ed.). *World Christian Encyclopaedia*. Oxford: OUP, 1982.

Costas, Orlando. *The Church and its Mission*. Wheaton: Tyndale House, 1974.

Cotterell, Peter. *Church Alive*. Leicester: IVP, 1981.

Gibbs, Eddie. *I Believe in Church Growth*. London: Hodder & Stoughton, 1981.

McGavran, Donald. *Understanding Church Growth*. Grand Rapids: Eerdmans, 1980.

Newbigin, Lesslie. *Open Secret*. London: SPCK, 1979.

Pointer, Roy. *How Do Churches Grow?* (Revised Edition) London: MARC Europe, 1987.

South Korea

Vincent, Eileen. *God Can Do It Here*. Basingstoke: Marshalls, 1982.

USA

Wagner, C. Peter. *Your Church Can Grow*. Glendale: Regal, 1976.

Wagner, C. Peter. *Church Growth and the Whole Gospel*. London: MARC Europe, 1987.

United Kingdom

Forster, Roger (ed.). *Ten New Churches*. London: MARC Europe, 1986.

Gibbs, Eddie. *Followed or Pushed?* London: MARC Europe, 1987.

Gibbs, Eddie (ed.). *Ten Growing Churches*. London: MARC Europe, 1985.

Harris, Jeffrey. *Can British Methodism Grow Again?* London: Methodist, 1981.

MacRae, Andrew. *Your Church Must Choose*. London: Pickering & Inglis, 1983.

Gifts and Groups

Bridge, D. and Phypers, D. *Spiritual Gifts and the Church*. Leicester: IVP, 1973.

Griffiths, Michael. *Cinderella with Amnesia*. Leicester: IVP, 1973.

———. Serving Grace. London: MARC Europe, 1986.

Hestenes, Roberta *Using the Bible in Groups*. Swindon: Bible Society, 1983.

Snyder, Howard. *New Wineskins*. Basingstoke: Marshalls, 1975.

———. Community of the King. Leicester: IVP, 1977.

Wagner, C. Peter. *Your Spiritual Gifts Can Help Your Church Grow*. London: MARC Europe, 1985.

Evangelism

Aldrich, Joseph. *Lifestyle Evangelism*. Basingstoke: Marshalls, 1984.

Brown, Colin. *That You May Believe*. Grand Rapids: Eerdmans, 1986.

Calver, Copley, Moffatt and Smith. *A Guide to Evangelism*. Basingstoke: Marshalls, 1984.

Engel, James. *Contemporary Christian Communications*. Nashville: Thomas Nelson, 1979.

——— and Norton. *What's Gone Wrong with the Harvest?* Grand Rapids: Zondervan, 1975.

Green, Michael. *Evangelism in the Early Church*. London: Hodder & Stoughton, 1970.

Packer, J. I. *Evangelism and the Sovereignty of God*. Leicester: IVP, 1961.

Stott, John. *Christian Mission in the Modern World*. London: Falcon, 1975.

Wimber, John. *Power Evangelism*. London: Hodder & Stoughton, 1985.

Planning for Growth

Cormack, David. *Seconds Away!* London: MARC Europe, 1986.

—— *Team Spirit.* London: MARC Europe, 1987.

Dayton, Edward. *God's Purpose, Man's Plans.* Monrovia: MARC, 1974.

—— and Engstrom. *Strategy for Leadership.* London: MARC Europe, 1985.

Minear, Paul S. *Images of the Church in the New Testament.* Cambridge: Lutterworth, 1961.

What Is World Vision?

World Vision is a major Christian relief and development agency, founded over 35 years ago. World Vision now helps the hungry, the homeless, the sick and the poor in over 80 countries worldwide.

World Vision is international, interdenominational and has no political affiliation, working wherever possible through local churches and community leaders in close cooperation with the United Nations and other international relief agencies.

Childcare sponsorship is an important part of World Vision's Christian work. Over 400,000 children are currently being cared for in over 3,500 projects.

Sponsors in Europe and around the world are helping thousands of needy children by supplying food, clothing, medical care and schooling. These children usually live with their families although some are in schools or homes. Development and training are usually offered to the communities where the sponsored children live so that whole families can become self-reliant.

World Vision is able to respond with immediate and appropriate relief in crisis situations such as famines, floods, earthquakes and wars. Hundreds of thousands have been saved in Africa through feeding and medical centres. Other projects include cyclone relief for Bangladesh, relief work in Lebanon and medical assistance for Kampuchea.

Over 500 community development projects in 50 countries are helping people to help themselves towards a healthier and more stable future. These projects include agricultural and vocational training, improvements in health care and nutrition (especially for mothers and babies), instruction in hygiene, literacy classes for children and adults, development of clean water supplies and village leadership training.

World Vision's approach to aid is integrated in the sense that we believe in helping every aspect of a person's life and needs. We also help Christian leaders throughout the world to become more effective in their ministry and assist local churches in many lands with their work.

If you would like more information about the work of World Vision, please contact one of the offices listed below:

World Vision of Britain
Dychurch House
8 Abington Street
Northampton
NN1 2AJ, United Kingdom
Tel: 0604 22964

World Vision of Australia
Box 399–C, G P O
Melbourne, 3001 Victoria
Australia
Tel: 3 699 8522

World Vision Deutschland
Postfach 1848
Adenauerallee 32
D-6370 Oberursel
West Germany
Tel: 6171 56074/5/6/7

World Vision International
Christliches Hilfswerk
Mariahilferstr 10/10
A-1070 Wien
Austria
Tel: 222–961 333/366

World Vision International
Christliches Hilfswerk
Badenserstr 87
CH-8004 Zürich
Switzerland
Tel: 1–241 7222

World Vision of Ireland
38 Baggot Street
Dublin 4
Eire
Tel: 609432

World Vision Singapore
Maxwell Rd
PO Box 2878
Singapore 9048
Tel: 224–8037/7419

Suomen World Vision
Kalevankatu 14 C 13
00100 Helsinki 10
Finland
Tel: 90 603422

World Vision of New Zealand
PO Box 1923
Auckland
New Zealand
Tel: 9 770 879

Stichting World
Vision Nederland
Postbus 818
3800 AV Amersfoort
The Netherlands
Tel: 33 10041

World Vision Canada
6630 Turner Valley Rd
Mississauga, Ontario
Canada L5N 2S4
Tel: 416 821 3030

World Vision United States
919 West Huntington Drive
Monrovia
CA 91016
USA
Tel: 818 303 8811

World Vision of Hong Kong
PO Box 98580
Tsim Sha Tsui Post Office
Kowloon
Hong Kong
Tel: 3–7221634

World Vision of Southern Africa
PO Box 1101
Florida 1710
South Africa
Tel: 674–2043/6/9

Co-publishers

MARC Europe is an integral part of World Vision, an international Christian humanitarian organisation. MARC's object is to assist Christian leaders with factual information surveys, management skills, strategic planning and other tools for evangelism. MARC Europe also publishes and distributes related books on matters of mission, church growth, management, spiritual maturity and other topics.

The British Church Growth Association is a coordinating body for those interested in the growth (spiritual, numerical, organic and incarnational) of the British Church today. It comprises researchers, teachers, consultants and practitioners who share information, insights, experience, and new thinking through regional and national activities, a regular journal, occasional publications and other resources, seminars and conferences. It is based at St Mark's Chambers, Kennington Park Road, London SE11 4PW.

BMMF Interserve is an international, interdenominational evangelical mission with 350 members in 10 countries of South Asia and the Middle East – along with several serving among Asian ethnic groups in Britain. It is voluntarily supported, and staffed by Christians both from Asia and from the West. Its aim is to meet human need with the love of God and the Gospel of Christ. To this end, it is set on a course of steady expansion to take up the invitations and opportunities presented to it.

British Church Growth Association

The British Church Growth Association was formed in September 1981 by a widely representative group of Christians committed to church growth either as researchers, teachers, practitioners or consultants. Following the Lausanne Congress on World Evangelisation in 1974, much interest was aroused in Church Growth thinking, which in turn led to the first UK Church Growth Consultation in 1978. Also during the 1970's a number of denominations had taken some church growth thinking and developed it within their own networks. A number of theological colleges and Bible colleges also began to teach church growth theory, particularly in their missiology departments. The Bible Society had begun to develop church growth courses that were being received enthusiastically. Developments in the work of the Evangelical Alliance led to the setting up of a Church Growth Unit and the publication of a *Church Growth Digest*. This unit drew together a number of leaders involved in the church growth field, but it was agreed to widen its impact by the formation of an association which would be even more comprehensive and effective.

Definition

Church Growth investigates the nature, function, structure, health and multiplication of Christian churches as they relate to the effective implementation of Christ's commission to "Go then to all peoples everywhere and make them my disciples" (Matt. 28:19). Church Growth seeks to combine the revealed truths of the Bible with related insights from the contemporary social and behavioural sciences. Although not linked to any one school of

church growth it owes much to the formational thinking of Dr
Donald McGavran.

Aims

The BCGA aims to help and encourage the Church in Britain to
move into growth in every dimension. The facilities and resources
of the BCGA are available to researchers, consultants, teachers,
practitioners and those just setting out in church growth thinking.
The Association endeavours to offer practical help as well as
encouraging and initiating Church Growth thinking and research.

Activities

The following are among its activities:
— Producing a quarterly journal particularly geared to the
  British scene with practical, biblical and theoretical articles
  of help to the churches as well as offering a forum for the
  sharing of views.
— Producing a number of occasional in-depth papers on a variety
  of topics.
— Co-publishing books on Church Growth.
— Running a specialist Church Growth book service offering
  discounted books to members and producing a catalogue of
  recommended church growth reading.
— Operating a reference system for information and personnel.
— Organising biennial residential conferences on particular
  topics of Church Growth relevant to the church in this
  country e.g. Church Planting 1983, Conversion 1985, Bridge
  Building 1987.
— Encouraging, co-ordinating or organising lectures and
  seminars on particular subjects or with particular speakers
  which could be of help to the churches.
— Carrying out research in allied fields and building up a
  research register of work already done or being undertaken
  in various centres.
— Monitoring church growth at home and overseas.
— Linking in with a European initiative to share insights peculiar to the continent of Europe.
— Encouraging grass-roots involvement through seventeen
  regional groups.

Government

The Council of the BCGA is made up of 15 elected members and 7 co-opted members who meet 3 times a year. Although members serve in a personal capacity, the Council aims to be representative of geographical region, denomination and churchmanship, practitioner, researcher and teacher.

The day-to-day running of the Association is carried out by an officer with some secretarial assistance and the active support of members of the Council. The offices are situated in St Marks Chambers, Kennington Park Road, London SE11 4PW and the telephone number is 01-793-0264. The BCGA is a registered charity, no. 28557.

Membership

Membership of the BCGA is open to both individuals and organisations interested in or involved in the theory or practice of Church Growth. On payment of an annual subscription members are entitled to receive the *Church Growth Digest* (the journal of the Association) four times a year, information about activities through the Newsletters, special discounts on conferences and books, membership of the Church Growth Book Service, voting rights to elect members to the Council every two years, links with other researchers, teachers, practitioners, end consultants on a regional or national level as well as help or advice on allied matters.

The current subscription is £8 for individual membership and £17 for organisations or churches.

Further information about the Association and membership is available from the Secretary, British Church Growth Association, St Mark's Chambers Kennington Park Road, London SE11 4PW.